ANIMAL STATS

CREEPY CRAWLERS

SIMON ABBOTT

Enslow PUBLISHING

Published in 2027 by Enslow Publishing, LLC
2544 Clinton Street
Buffalo, NY 14224

First published in Great Britain in 2025 by Wayland

Printed in China

CPSIA compliance information: Batch #QS27ENS: For further information contact Enslow Publishing LLC, New York, New York at 1-800-398-2504.

Please visit our website, www.enslowpublishing.com. For a free color catalog of all our high-quality books, call toll free 1-800-398-2504 or fax 1-877-980-4454.

Cataloging-in-Publication Data

Names: Abbott, Simon, 1967-.
Title: Creepy crawlers / Simon Abbott.
Description: Buffalo, NY : Enslow Publishing, 2027. |
Series: Animal stats | Includes glossary.
Identifiers: ISBN 9781978549296 (pbk.) | ISBN 9781978549302 (library bound) | ISBN 9781978549319 (ebook)
Subjects: LCSH: Invertebrates--Juvenile literature. | Insects--Juvenile literature.
Classification: LCC QL362.4 A34 2027 | DDC 592--dc23

Find us on

CONTENTS

STEP INTO THE
INCREDIBLE WORLD OF ANIMAL STATS!

Welcome to the fascinating world of bugs and minibeasts.

With an estimated **1.4 billion*** insects for every human on Earth, it's important that we get to know them!

*This number is approximate.
Minibeasts don't stay still long enough to get an accurate count!

Bugs and minibeasts can be found in almost any environment – from under a rock in the park to a pool of water at the seaside, from a snowy mountain to a scorching desert, even in the freezing Arctic!

Turn the page to uncover spiders as large as dinner plates, bumblebees that fly as high as Mount Everest, and record-breaking migrating butterflies.

SO GRAB YOUR MAGNIFYING GLASS
AND JOIN US AS WE EXPLORE
MINIBEAST MEASUREMENTS
AND INSECT INFO!

INSECT INFO

Counting all the minibeasts on Earth would be a never-ending task, but experts estimate that there are approximately **10 quintillion (10,000,000,000,000,000,000)** individual insects sharing our planet.

It's believed that bugs and minibeasts make up an astonishing **80%** of all living species on Earth, and their combined weight is around **70 times** more than the entire human population!

Entomologists (which is the name given to people who study insects) have identified over **one million** different species. But who knows? There could be **nine million** more creepy crawlies just waiting to be discovered!

WHY WE NEED MINIBEASTS

Bugs and insects play an essential role in maintaining balance within every ecosystem. They pollinate plants, produce valuable resources such as honey, wax, fabric, and medicine, control harmful crop pests, and even serve as a food source themselves.

Insects can be divided into four main groups, or orders. Take a look!

ORDER	NUMBER OF SPECIES	EXAMPLES	
Beetles (Coleoptera)	**300,000–400,000**	Ladybug Stag beetle	
Butterflies and Moths (Lepidoptera)	**180,000**	Monarch butterfly Gypsy moth	
True Flies (Diptera)	**150,000**	Mosquito Fruit fly	
Ants, wasps, and bees (Hymenoptera)	**150,000**	Bullet ant Honey bee	

Insects can be found in every corner and crevice of the planet, but there is only one that is native to Antarctica – it's a wingless midge called **Belgica antarctica**.

Imagine this! If you put ALL the creatures on Earth in a line,

Four out of every **five** animals would be minibeasts or invertebrates (small creatures without backbones).

But how can we begin to identify them? This chart might help:

GROUP: ARTHROPODS

84% of creatures fall into this animal classification.

Some live on land, some are aquatic, and others can fly. As well as insects, bugs, and minibeasts, you can find crabs, lobsters, and shrimp in this group too!

Sub-group of arthropods:

INSECTS

6 jointed legs

Exoskeleton

2 antennae

3 body parts: head, thorax, abdomen

0-2 pairs of wings

EXAMPLE: Dragonfly

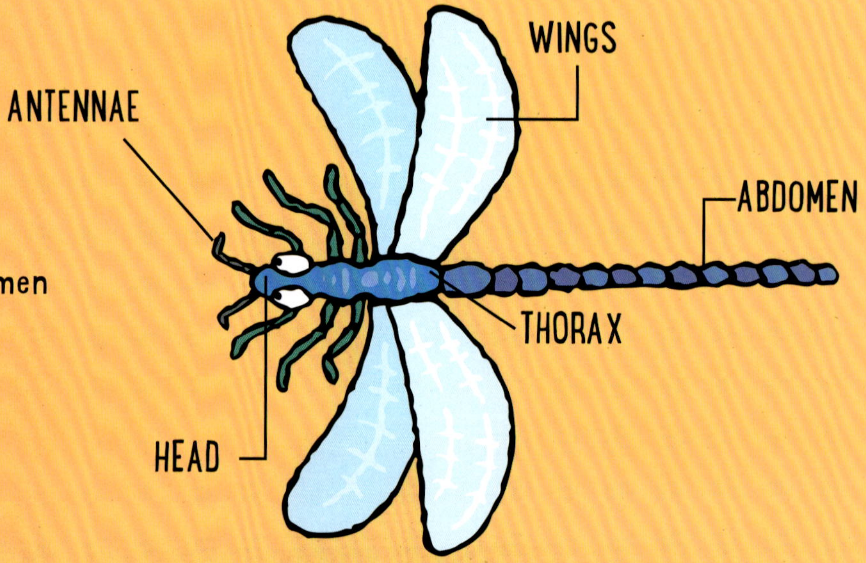

Sub-group of arthropods:

ARACHNIDS

8 jointed legs

Exoskeleton

No antennae

2 body parts: a fused head and thorax called a **cephalothorax**, and an abdomen

No wings

EXAMPLE: Spider

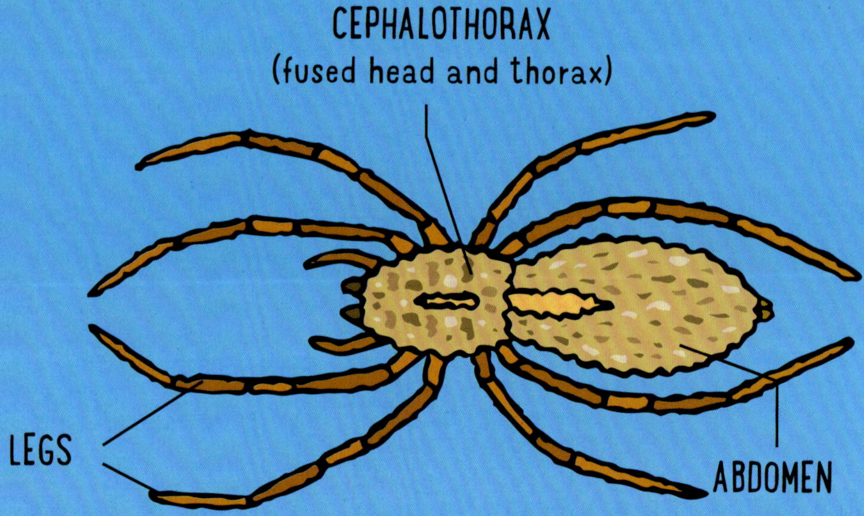

Sub-group of arthropods:
MYRIAPOD
Lots of legs
Exoskeleton
Many body parts
2 antennae

EXAMPLE: Centipede

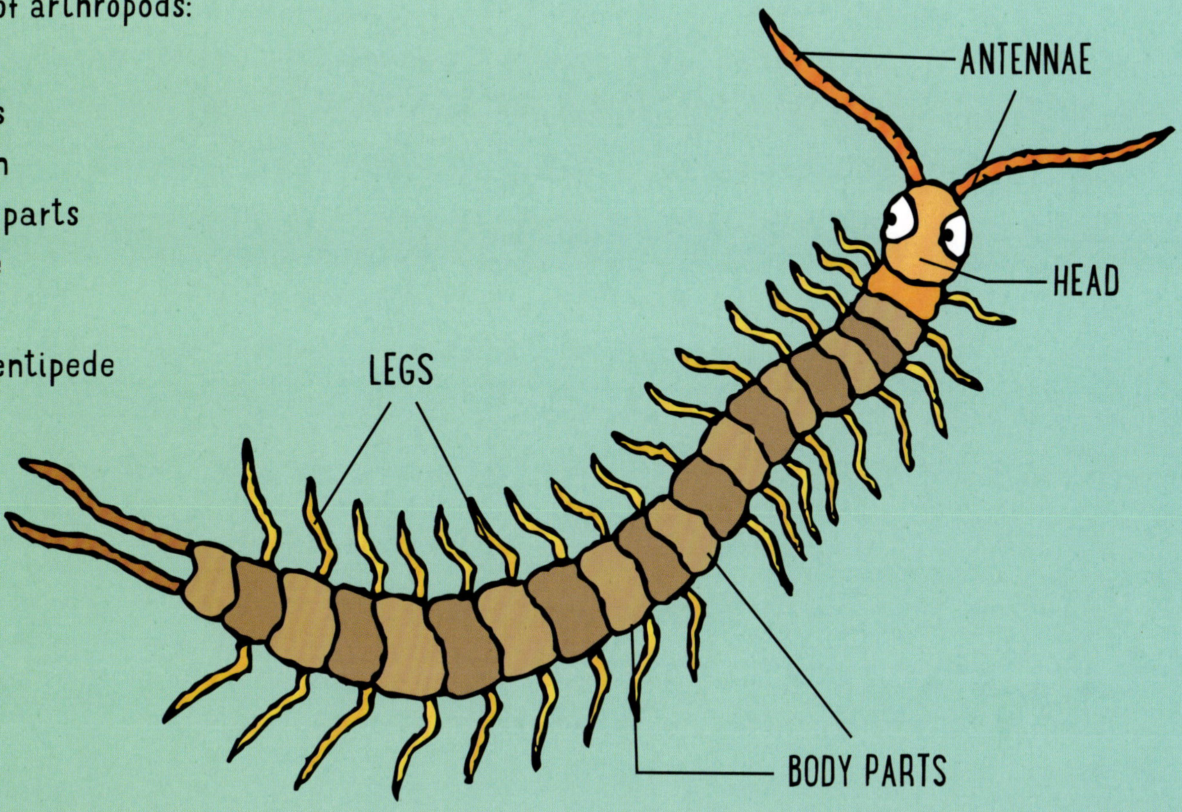

Sub-group of arthropods:
CRUSTACEAN
Usually 10-14 jointed legs
Exoskeleton
4 antennae

EXAMPLE: Woodlouse

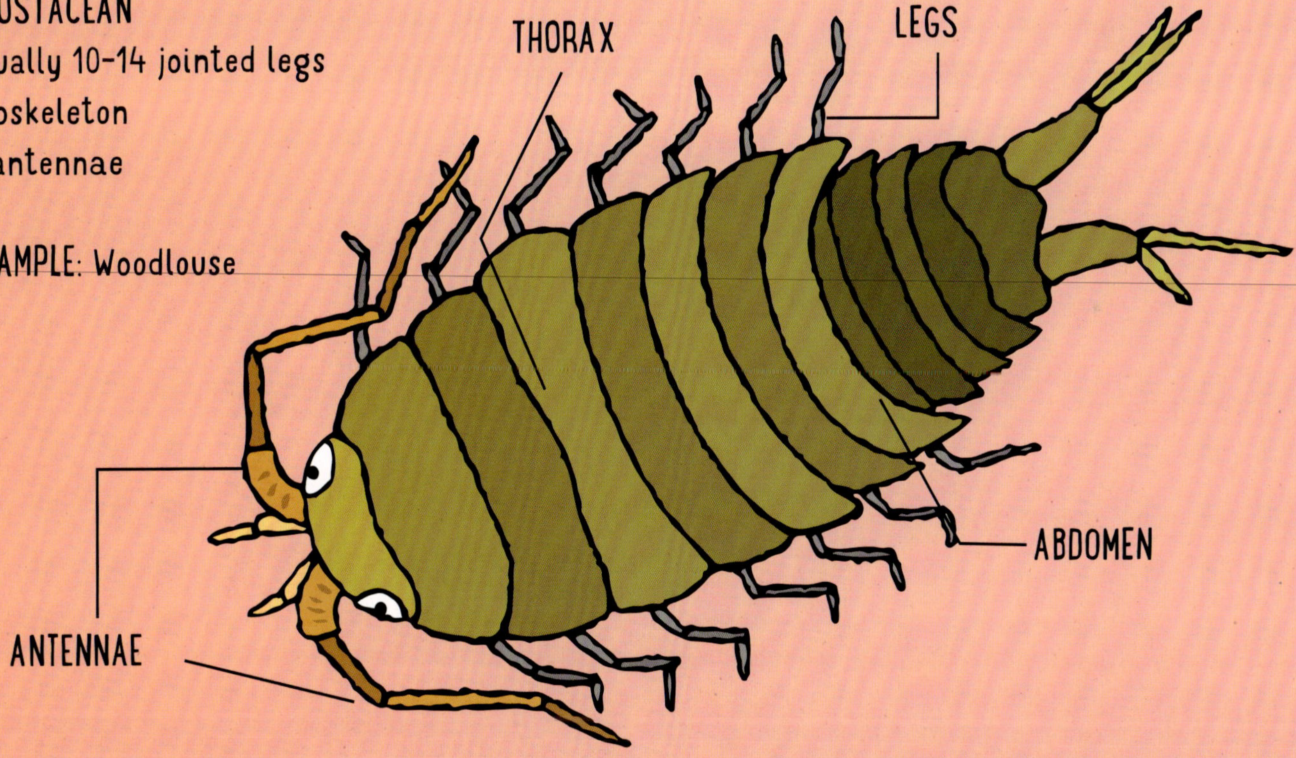

GROUP:

MOLLUSKS

The soft body has 3 main parts: the head, visceral hump, and foot

Many mollusks have a shell

EXAMPLE: Snail

GROUP:

ANNELIDS

They have a soft, segmented body

EXAMPLE: Worm

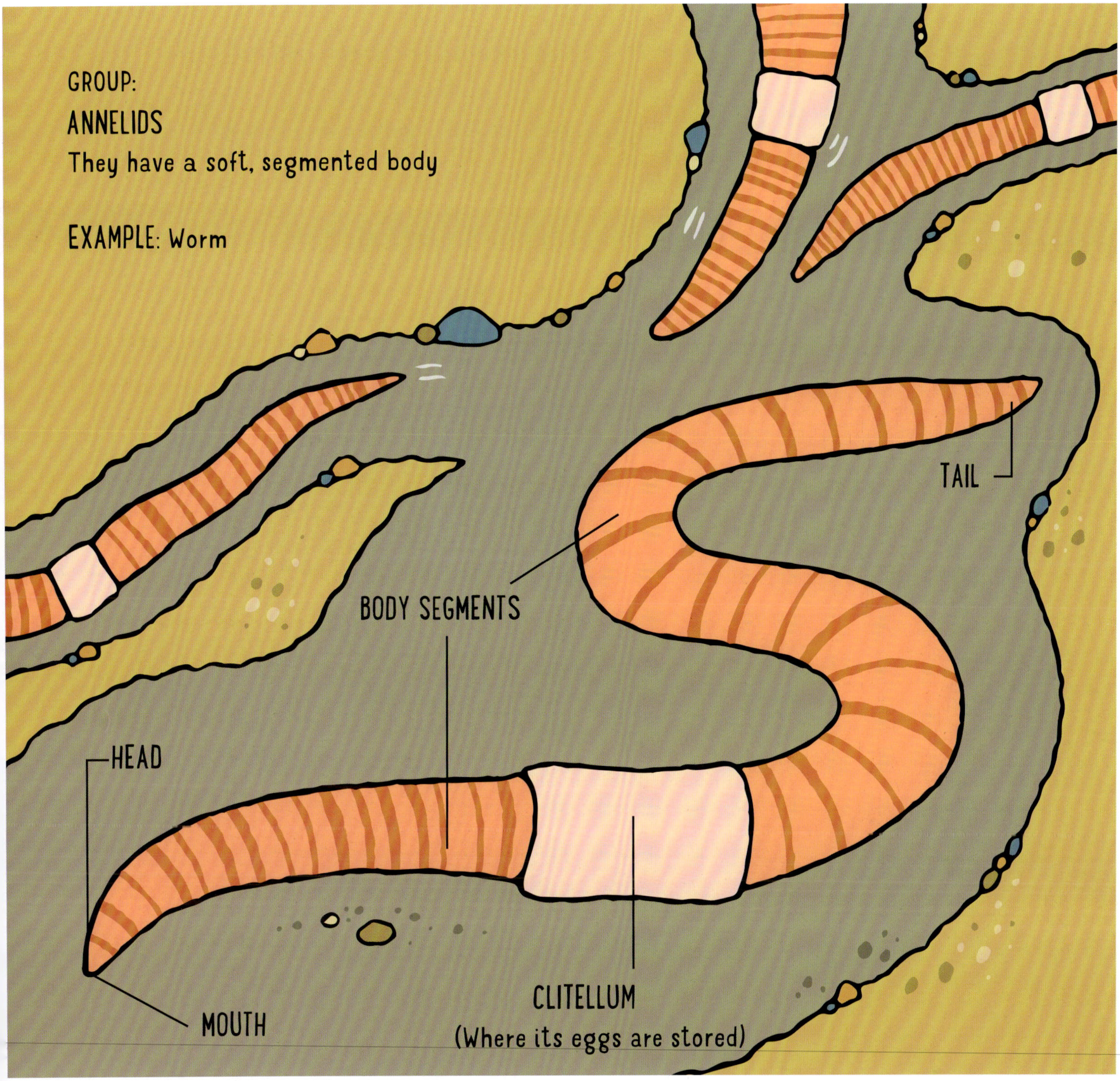

The term "**exoskeleton**" literally translates to "outside skeleton." It acts as an armor, providing protection and support for the insect's soft body. When the creature's internal body grows, the exoskeleton is shed and is replaced by a new one. This process is known as **molting**.

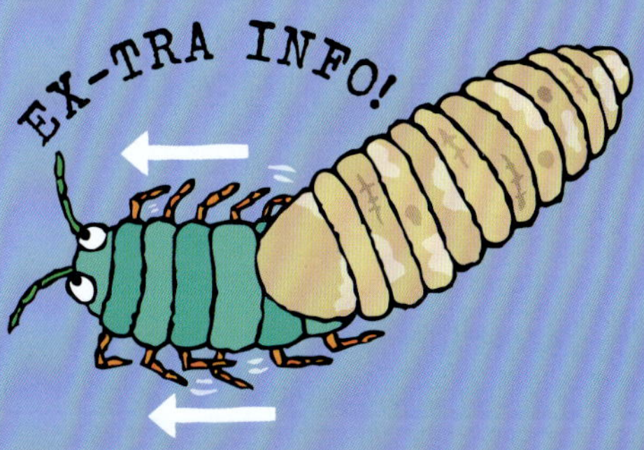

FLYING FOSSILS

For over **480 million** years, insects have been hopping, buzzing, and crawling across our planet. They were the first creatures to take to the skies, dominating Earth for **250 million** years before dinosaurs even existed.

But how did these ancient insects differ from the ones we know today? Picture a **dragonfly** with wings as wide as a tennis racket is high or a **millipede** longer than your bed!

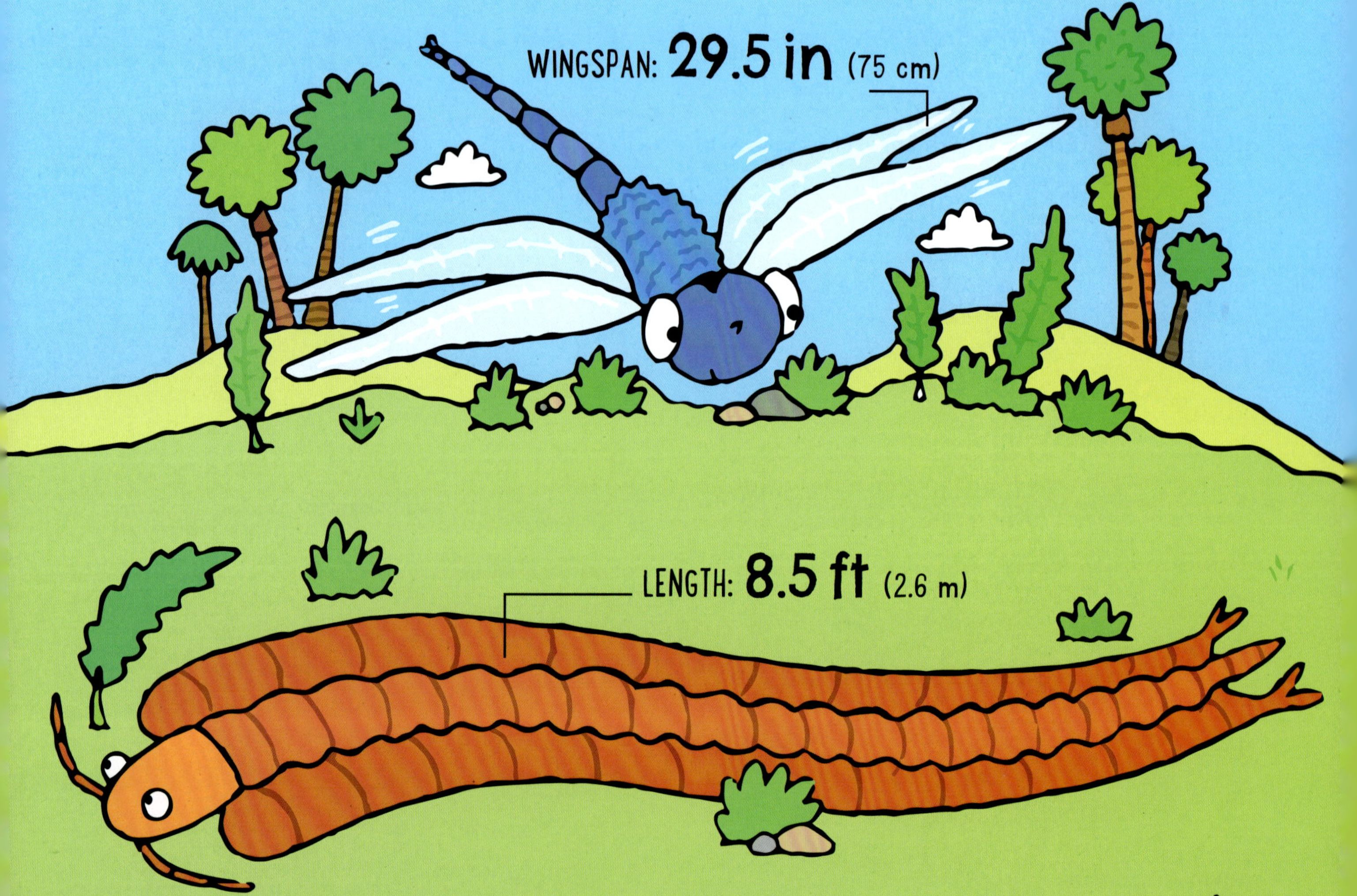

Why did these bugs grow so big?

It's thought that the prehistoric atmosphere contained **50%** more oxygen than it does today. Oxygen in large amounts can be poisonous. One way to reduce this danger is to grow larger: smaller amounts of the gas is absorbed relative to their body size.

How do we know so much about these prehistoric bugs?

Scientists can study fossilized remains that are
99 million years old
and trapped in hardened tree bark resin, known as amber. Incredible!

The oldest insect ever discovered is the fossilized ***Rhyniognatha hirsti***, which crawled around over **400 million** years ago in what is now Aberdeen, Scotland. Some prehistoric species of insects, such as silverfish, mayflies, wasps, and spiders are still thriving today.

GET UP AND GROW

Let's move on from old fossils to brand-new bugs!
Where does an insect's journey begin?

Most minibeasts emerge from tiny, soft-shell **eggs**, laid by the female insect.

AMAZING MOMS!

The **African driver ant** can lay a staggering **four million** eggs every **25** days.

In Australia, a **ghost moth** was observed laying **29,100** eggs in a single sitting!

Most insects go through **two** different types of life cycles:

INCOMPLETE METAMORPHOSIS

This has three simple stages:

EXAMPLE: **Dragonfly**

1 EGGS

The female adult lays **eggs** in or near water.

2 NYMPH

The nymph, or larva, can hunt near water. Nymphs shed their **exoskeleton** several times as they grow.

3 ADULT

Their **wings** are fully developed. They can fly to find food and a mate.

Other examples include crickets, grasshoppers, and cockroaches.

COMPLETE METAMORPHOSIS

This has four simple stages:

EXAMPLE: **Butterfly**

EGGS

Laid by a **female butterfly** onto, or near, a food plant.

2 CATERPILLAR (LARVA)

Feeds on leaves and grows quickly. Hangs upside down to form the **chrysalis**.

3 CATERPILLAR (PUPA)

A hard-covering forms around the chrysalis.
It undergoes metamorphosis and squeezes out as an adult butterfly.

4 ADULT BUTTERFLY

The female lays eggs.

The longest recorded lifespan of an insect is held by a **queen ant** (*Lasius niger*), with an impressive **28¾** years.

At the other end of the scale, **mayflies** have the shortest lifespan of any animal, with only a brief **24** hours to enjoy and experience life on Earth.

SUPER SENSES

Bugs and insects have some of the best senses in the animal kingdom. Let's explore how minibeasts use their senses of sight, smell, taste, touch, and hearing.

An insect's eye is made up of **thousands** of tiny light-focusing detectors tightly squashed together. This helps them to spot things to eat, alerts them to sudden attacks, and gives them superwide vision.

For instance, a large dragonfly can have up to **30,000** lenses in each **compound eye**, providing them with nearly **360°** vision from all angles.

I-SPY WITH MY LITTLE EYE!

The male horsefly has holoptic eyes, which means its **two** eyeballs merge at the top of its head. This unique structure allows one section of the eye to detect distant flying insects, while the other is excellent with close-up details. How perfect!

DID YOU KNOW?

Some butterflies have **15** different types of photoreceptors in their eyes, compared to humans' **two**. This enables them to see **two** different types of light that humans cannot see. The first is **polarized light**, which is reflected from another butterfly's colorful wings. This helps them to find a potential mate. The second is ultraviolet (UV) light, which is displayed in flowers and makes it easy for butterflies to spot nectar.

Most spiders have **eight** eyes, in **two** rows. However, the *sinopoda scurion* spider, which lives in a river cave in China, has no eyes at all! (I suppose there's not much point having eyes if the cave is in total darkness!)

Insects rely on tiny receptors found on their antennae, called sensilla, to detect odors in the air. The more antennae an insect has, the stronger its sense of smell will be.

The insect world's smell-superstar is the **male silk moth**. This creature's antennae are so tuned in to the female's chemical signals (called **pheromones**) that it can track a potential mate from up to **30 miles** (48 km) away!

A close second is the jewel beetle that can sniff out a burning pine tree **10 miles** (16 km) away.

THAT'S NOT TO BE SNIFFED AT!

For a while, scientists believed that **dragonflies** and **damselflies** had no sense of smell. But a research team found evidence that the small bulbs on their antennae actually send out nerve signals when they detect the scent of their favorite snack – fruit flies!

You and I have taste buds on our tongues. Insects have taste sensillas which usually look like tiny hairs, called **pegs**. A fruit fly, for instance, has over **680** sensillas. Insects can detect **five** different tastes: sour, salty, bitter, a savory flavor called umami, and their favorite, sweet! Their pegs can also be used to sense potential mates, spot suitable egg-laying locations, and identify the parts of their bodies that need cleaning. You can find these tiny hairs all over an insect's body.

WHAT A FEAT!

An insect can use its feet to figure out if something is good enough to eat.

In a similar way, when a female butterfly stands on a plant, she can detect if the leaf will make an ideal habitat for her eggs, and a tasty food source for the soon-to-be born caterpillars.

Listen up! As insects move through their environment, or ecosystem, they need to make sense of sounds in order to communicate and listen out for predators.

When insects first appeared on the planet **400 million** years ago, they were deaf. As they have evolved, some insects have developed the ability to "hear" in various ways:

Tympanal organs are found in some insects and act as an eardrum. They catch soundwaves in the air which are decoded by **sensory cells**, then **neurons** send signals to the insect's brain.

A male mosquito's "ear" has **15,000** of these neurons!

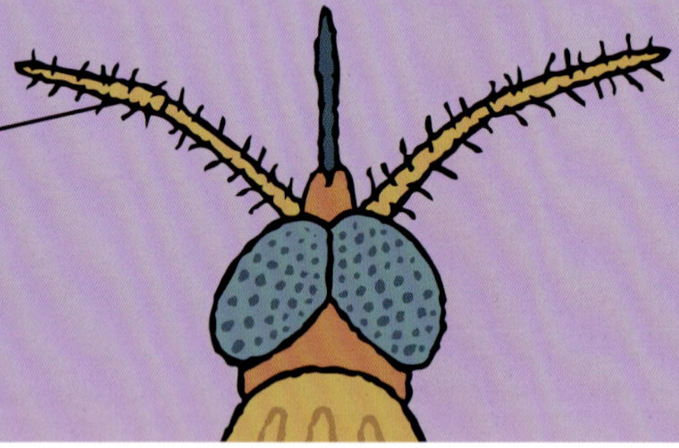

Mosquitoes and fruit flies use a group of **sensory cells** on the second segment of their antennae to sense vibrations.

Grasshoppers, crickets, and butterfly larvae are among the minibeasts that sense sound vibrations using small, stiff hairs called **setae**.

A caterpillar reacts to these sonic beats by getting into defensive mode. Some will become motionless, but others will rise up and get ready for a scuffle!

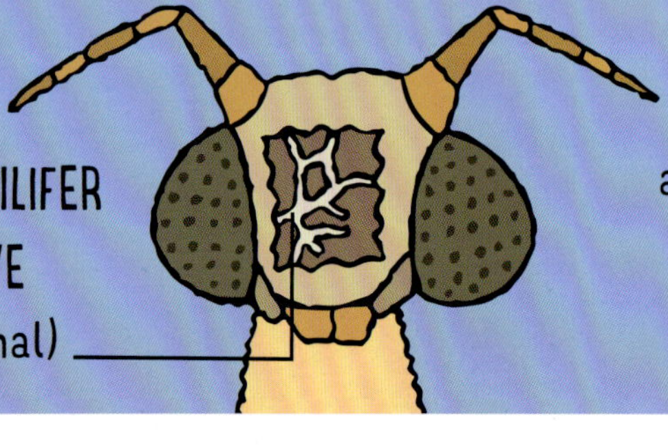

Hawkmoths have a tiny hair-like organ in their mouth called a **labral pilifer**, which allows them to detect **ultrasonic** sounds from predatory bats and avoid capture.

Spiders don't have ears like you and me – they rely on nerve-based receptors on their legs! Some species have a remarkable ability to hear a variety of sounds from distances of over **6 feet** (1.8 m). The spider's receptors detect soundwaves, then communicate these vibrations to their brain.

The **ogre-faced spider** is a sense-superstar and can identify both low frequency sounds of insect wings and high-pitched calls from predatory birds from almost **6.5 feet** (2 m) away! And guess what? Their ability to see in the dark is **2,000** times better than a human's! A real sense-superstar!

A **snail** is supersensitive to touch, with special **cells** from its head to its foot. If a snail feels under threat, it can withdraw its eye stalks at lightning speed, then retreat into its shell using its powerful **retractor muscle**.

WONDER WORM!

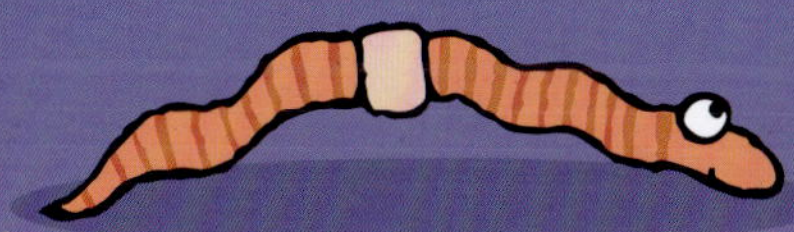

Without eyes or ears, an **earthworm** relies on its sense of touch to survive. It can feel different textures, detect light and dark, sense vibrations from predators, and taste chemicals in the soil with the special nerve cells that cover the length of the earthworm's body.

RECORD-BREAKING BUGS

Grab your ruler, scales, and stopwatch! You'll be amazed at the prizewinning bugs and minibeasts that have made their way into our record books!

WORLD'S LARGEST BUTTERFLY

Queen Alexandra's birdwing

This insect's wings are bigger than the height of this book!

WORLD'S LARGEST SPIDER

Goliath birdeater

This spider's leg span could easily cover your entire dinner plate!

WORLD'S LARGEST LAND SNAIL

African giant snail

One of these snails reached this whopping length, equivalent to two bananas lined up end-to-end!

The specimen with the longest body was a stick insect called (deep breath) **Chan's megastick *(Phobaeticus chani)***.

This creature, found in the rainforests of Borneo, reached an astonishing length of **22.3 inches** (56.6 cm) when its legs were stretched out. Imagine over five toilet rolls end-to-end!

WORLD'S LARGEST CATERPILLAR

Hickory horned devil

These caterpillars be up to **5.5 inches** (14 cm) long, about the size of a hot dog.

WORLD'S LARGEST BEETLE

Hercules beetle

Including its plier-like horns, this colossal creature is **20** times the size of a ladybug at **7.5 inches** (19 cm)!

If it's down to body length alone, then the **Titan beetle** grabs first prize. At **6.6 inches** (16.7 cm), this bug is longer than an average smartphone!

ITSY-BITSY INFO!

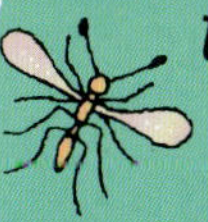

On the opposite end of the size spectrum, the tiniest known adult insect is a type of wasp called a **fairyfly**. These microscopic minibeasts measure just **0.03 inch** (0.75 mm) long – barely thicker than a sheet of paper!

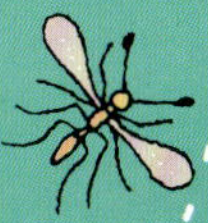

The superstrong **leafcutter ant** can lift and transport in its jaw something that's **50 times** its own bodyweight. To put this into perspective, it would be like a human lifting and carrying **six** polar bears with just their teeth! (Don't try that at home!)

The **WORLD'S HEAVIEST INSECT** title belongs to a type of grasshopper called the **giant weta**. This bulky bug topped the scales at **2.5 ounces** (71 g).

The froghopper is the insect

WORLD'S HIGH-JUMP CHAMPION.

It can leap an astonishing **100 times** its own body length thanks to a unique catapult-like mechanism in its body.

Now, that would be handy to have!

There's a real buzz around the **HIGH-FLYER** award!

The **alpine bumblebee** has been observed flying at heights of **2 miles** (3.25 km) above sea level. This bug can adapt its flying style to keep its wings moving in the thin mountain air. In fact, researchers have worked out that these insects could endure altitudes of **5.6 miles** (9 km) - that's higher than Mount Everest.

The **FIRST-CLASS FLUTTERING** prize goes to the **Forcipomyia midge** who can clock-up an exhausting **62,760** wing beats per minute.

In contrast, the **swallowtail butterfly** takes a more relaxed approach, achieving a more laid-back **300** beats per minute.

FLYING FACTS!

Locusts gather together in huge numbers to devour anything edible in their path. In 1874, an estimated **12.5 trillion** locusts formed a record-breaking swarm covering approximately **318,760 square miles** ($513,000\ km^2$) in the United States.

Measuring the flying speed of an insect is no easy task, but research suggests that **male horseflies** are the speediest of them all, buzzing after potential mates at a staggering **90 miles per hour** (145.8 km/h).

The land-speed record is held by an **Australian tiger beetle**, which can scuttle around at **5.5 miles per hour** (8.9 km/h). Is this slow? Let's look at the numbers.

AUSTRALIAN TIGER BEETLE	Runs at 171 body lengths per second to reach **5.5 mi/h** (8.9 km/h)
6-FOOT HUMAN	If they ran at 171 body lengths per second, they would be sprinting at **720 mi/h** (1,159 km/h) (nearly the speed of sound!)

THE INSECT ENDURANCE RECORD!

Each autumn, a staggering **29 million** painted lady butterflies embark on a daunting **8,700 miles** (14,000 km) round trip from Europe to the African savanna and back again! These intrepid insects battle over the Mediterranean Sea, North African mountains, and the Sahara, using favorable winds to help their journey along.

HIDE AND SEEK!

Insects use camouflage to creep up on prey and to hide from predators. The **flower mantis** is a master of disguise. It can mimic different flower types, copy the way petals flutter in the breeze, and can absorb UV light to attract UV-sensitive insects. Some species even look like twigs or decaying leaves.

The runner-up is the tiny **bird dropping spider** at **0.5 inch** (12 mm) long. Its black, brown, and white markings, combined with its ability to remain motionless, makes predators mistake this creepy-crawly for poo, rather than a juicy snack!

COPY CATS!

Some moths have evolved to copy other animals as a way to put off potential predators. There are moths that imitate spiders, wasps, frogs, and even owls!

The **GOLD MEDALIST** is the **hummingbird moth** – it looks and moves like a hummingbird and can even copy the distinctive hovering flight. These moths sip nectar through their long snout, which resembles the bird's unique beak.

DANGER! DANGER!

It's time for dinner! Let's learn about the art of catching and killing prey in a minibeast masterclass.

Assassin bugs are sneaky hunters. They are experts in camouflage, using dust, bark, and even decaying insects to hide while they ambush unsuspecting prey.

Assassin bugs have needle-like **mouthparts with three** segments that they use to inject poisonous saliva into their prey. The bug waits for its victim's body contents to liquify, then sucks out the dissolved innards. Job done!

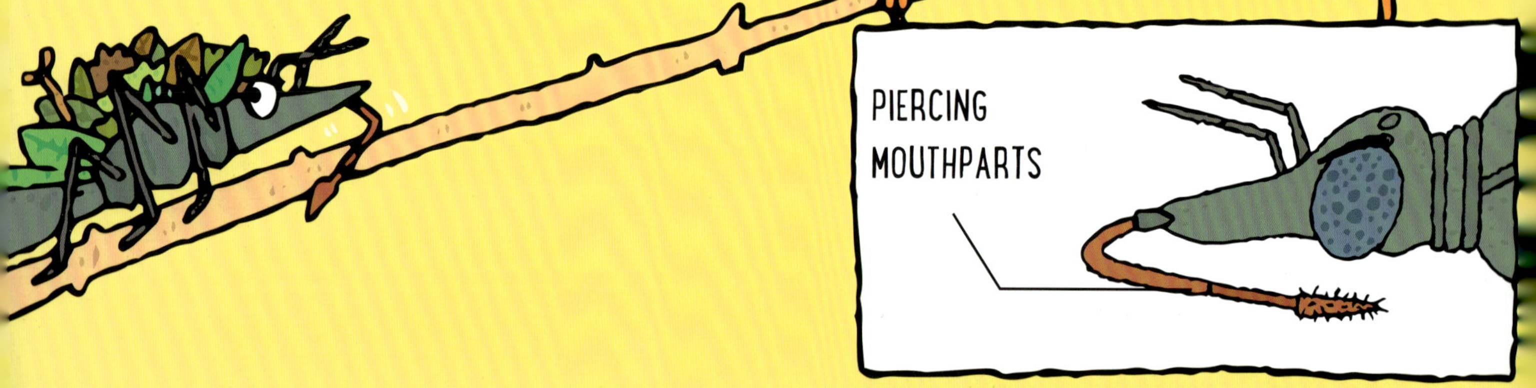

If it's an all-round predatory professional you're after, then look no further than the **praying mantis**. In just **milliseconds**, this tea-cup-sized insect can pounce on their prey and grip them with their strong forelegs and interlocking spines. Escape is out of the question!

The **Japanese hornet**, at **2 inches** (5 cm) long, is a ruthless hunter. It uses its razor-sharp jaws to behead its prey, then cuts its body into bite-sized pieces. The carcass is crunched into a soft paste that it feeds to the larvae back at the hornet's nest.

Japanese hornets can decimate a honeybee colony in a couple of hours, decapitating up to **30,000** bees one by one.

But don't underestimate **honeybees** – they have a clever defense mechanism against the Japanese hornet. When faced with this invasive predator, they will form a ball around it and vibrate their wing muscles for over an **hour** to create temperatures of up to **117°F** (47°C), which fries the invading hornet.

Luckily, a honeybee can survive temperatures up to **118-122°F** (48-50°C). Scientists have found that this kamikaze behavior does shorten the honeybee's life – but the hive comes first!

When your ecosystem is packed with predators, you need a top-notch defense system. To avoid being eaten, some insects have dramatic survival strategies.

The **bombardier beetle** can burst out a spray of toxic, burning-hot chemicals if predators get up close and personal. This battling bug can release **500** explosive blasts in a **single second!**

TOXIC TREATS!

If a predatory toad accidentally gobbles up a bombardier beetle, it can turn its stomach inside out to get rid of the explosive bug!

There are a number of **stinging caterpillars** that are covered in hollow hairs connected to tiny pockets of poison. These are used as defensive weapons and, when touched, the venom is released and could put you out of action for **12 hours!**

Some **caterpillars** will curl up into a ball and remain motionless until danger has passed. Others have developed whistling and clicking sounds to confuse predators such as birds and bats.

Ladybugs are hungry predators and can devour up to **5,000** aphids every year! But if the tables are turned, they have a trick up their sleeve. When threatened, they will let go of their host plant and crash to the ground, pretending to be dead until the predator goes away.

This behavior is known as **thanatosis**.

Stink bugs give off a revolting chemical odor when they feel under threat. Interestingly, they release a different smell when they find a safe place to hibernate to let their mates know the location!
They are great travelers too!
In 1998, they were found for the first time in the United States inside a fruit crate.
Just **20** years later, they had spread to **44** U.S. states and **4** Canadian provinces!

It might put your mind at rest to know that out of **50,000** spider species only **25** can harm humans. However, it's best to steer clear of the **funnel web spider**, as its bite can cause chaos in your nervous system, increase your heart rate, numb your mouth, and make breathing difficult.

The great news is that an **antivenom** has been available for the past **40 years**, and there hasn't been a funnel spider-based fatality since then.

A **parasite** is an organism that lives within or on another species, relying on its host for nutrients. The **loa loa worm** is a golf-tee-sized parasite that can live undiscovered in a human for years. But imagine your horror when one day you look in a mirror and spot a tiny worm wriggling in your own eyeball!

It's no wonder that this parasite has earned the nickname "**African eye worm**." Yuck!

The mosquito is **notorious** for its irritating "bites" and infamous for transmitting some of the deadliest diseases in the world, such as malaria and yellow fever.

Tragically, each year **600,000** people die from malaria, while **12,000** deaths are caused by yellow fever. This makes the mosquito the deadliest insect on the planet.

DID YOU KNOW?

Good news! New state-of-the-art mosquito nets that have been treated with insecticide have stopped an estimated **13 million** malaria cases and prevented **24,600** deaths.

VERY IMPORTANT INSECTS

If you thought that bugs and minibeasts just buzzed through life spoiling everyone's picnic, then think again – they have a critical role in our ecosystem!

Pollination is a vital part in the life cycle of plants. Let's take a look at how insects help the process along:

1 Insects are attracted to flowers by their sweet scent and colorful petals.

2 An insect lands on a flower to collect a sweet liquid called **nectar**.

3 While harvesting nectar, the insect brushes against the **anther** of the flower, where **pollen** is produced. Some of this pollen sticks to their body.

4 The insect buzzes off to another colorful flower.

5 As the insect feeds on the new flower's nectar, the pollen is deposited on the female part of the flower, called the **stigma**.

6 The pollen moves down to the **ovules** in the ovary. A process called **fertilization** happens, and a seed is developed.

A new plant is on the way!

So, why are pollinators so important to us? Well, without them we simply wouldn't survive. Of all the **1,400** crop plants grown around the world, almost **80%** need to be pollinated by animals. Unfortunately, insect pollinators are at risk due to factors such as climate change, loss of habitat, and use of pesticides.

Scientists estimate that there are **200,000-350,000** different animal species involved in pollination including birds, bats, beetles, and butterflies.

THE BEES' KNEES!

Bumblebees have a unique pollination method called **buzz pollination**, where they vibrate their hairy bodies to dislodge pollen that then gets collected in tiny baskets on their legs called corbiculae. Without bees, we would not have honey, apples, plums, pears, blueberries, squash, almonds, tomatoes, potatoes, strawberries, tea, coffee, or even chocolate!

TAKING CARE OF BUZZ-NESS!

A worker bee makes just **.03 ounce** (0.8 g) of honey in her lifetime, or **1/12th** of a teaspoon.

Around **1.9 million tons** (1.8 million mt) of honey is produced worldwide every year – imagine the weight of a blue whale, and a few jars on top!

As well as being a delicious spread on toast, **honey** also has medicinal properties as a natural antiseptic that can help heal burns, wounds, and infections.

It is also used in various products such as candles, lip balm, and skincare items.

Our ancestors have been pictured using honey in cave paintings dating back **8,000** years, and the ancient Egyptians used it to sweeten cakes, pay taxes and mummify their dead!

Shall we open the **silkworm** fact file? Firstly, it's not a worm at all – it's the larva or caterpillar of the ***Bombyx mori*** **moth**.

Silk has been made in China for the past **5,000** years, and the silk-making process was kept secret for **hundreds** of years.

Silkworms make their cocoon by rotating over **300,000** times in a figure-eight shape. The cocoon is made up of a single strand of silk that can be **3,000 feet** (900 m) long. Every year, the world's silkworm population produces over **220,000** tons (200,000 mt) of silk – that's the weight of **900** jumbo jets!

SURGERY STATS!

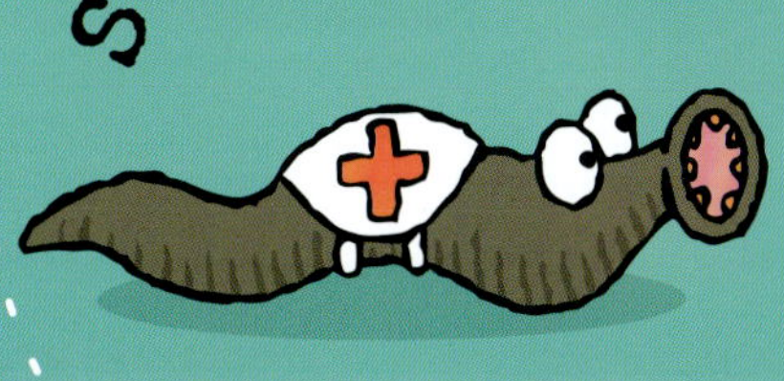

Leeches have been used as a medical aid for **thousands** of years, and they are making a comeback! Leeches pierce the patient's skin with their **100** teeth, then suck out blood while injecting something that prevents blood clots. Leeches have been approved to aid recovery in reconstructive surgery, blocked arteries, and varicose veins.

Are you familiar with the term "entomophagy"?

It simply refers to the practice of eating insects. Have you crunched on a cricket, munched on a millipede or licked a larva lollipop?

Two billion people in **80%** of countries around the world include insects in their diets, and there are over **2,000** known species of edible bugs.

Let's take a food journey around the globe:

AUSTRALIA

Roasted cockroaches and honey-flavored ants

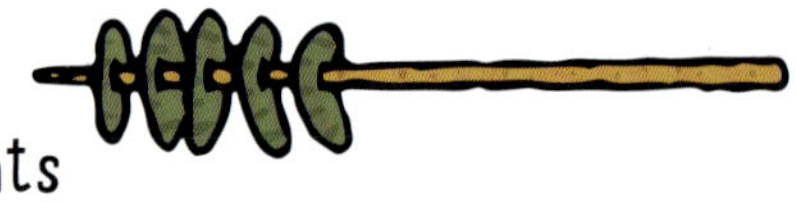

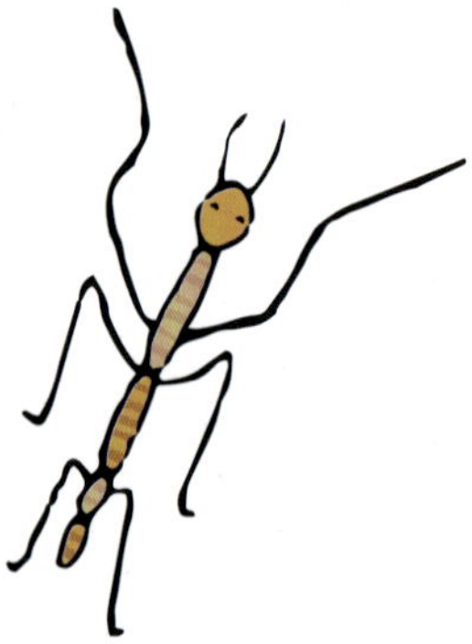

BRAZIL

Ant burgers and fried tarantulas

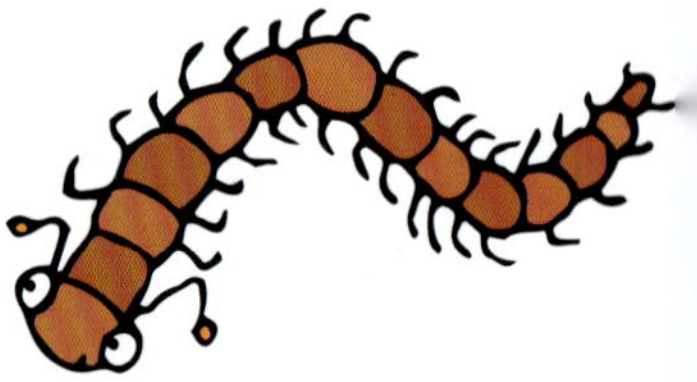

CHINA

Over **300** species of insects are eaten here, including bee cocoons and roasted larvae

COLOMBIA

Fat-bottomed ants, which taste like bacon with a dash of lime

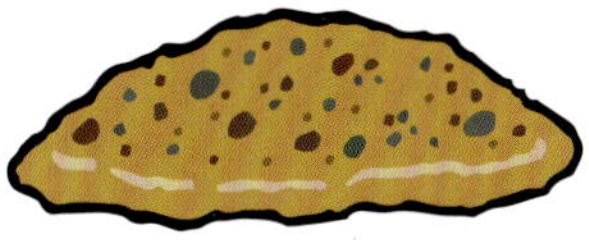

FINLAND

A unique bread containing around **70** dried crickets in the dough.

JAPAN

You can buy bugs in cans from vending machines!

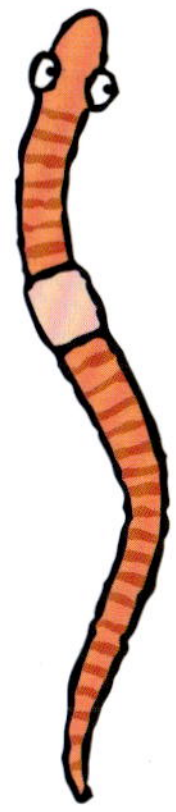

MEXICO

Grasshoppers in tacos

NETHERLANDS

Chocolate with mealworms

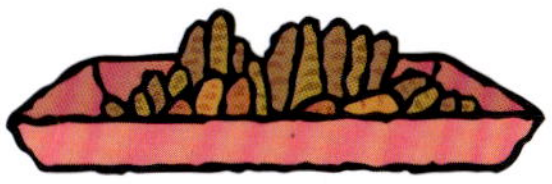

SOUTH AFRICA

Fried mopane worms and chocolate-covered locusts

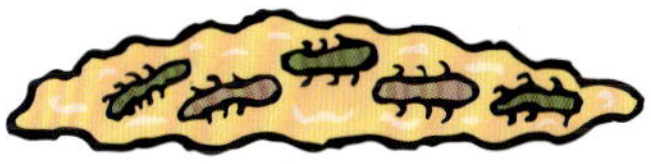

THAILAND

Cricket omelette

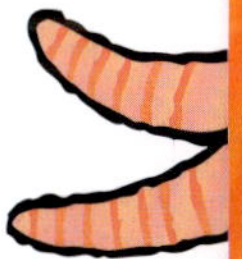

Why is **entomophagy**, or bug-eating, such a hot topic? It's estimated that the world's population will reach **10 billion** by 2050, so finding sustainable and nutritious food sources for everyone will be a challenge. **Entomophagy** could hold the solution.

88% of an insect is edible, compared with **40%** of pork or beef. They are high in protein, fatty acids, vitamins, fiber, and essential minerals. Less land and food is required to cultivate insects compared to traditional meat sources. Bugs produce fewer greenhouse gases and thrive on organic waste.

DELICIOUS DATA

Emperor Hirohito of Japan (1901-1989) was a fan of **entomophagy** and his favorite dish was fried wasps with boiled rice, sugar, and soy sauce!

CREEPY-CRAWLY CRASH PADS

Insect habitats are found in every corner of the planet, from hot deserts to ice floes, tropical rainforests to mountain tops. Let's pay a visit to some of the places bugs call home.

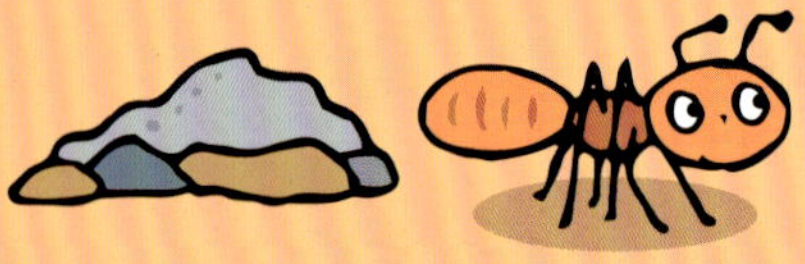

Ants are social creatures that live in colonies, sometimes with up to **20,000** other ants. These colonies have a highly organized structure, and the ants work together to gather food, reproduce, protect their **queen**, and defend their territory.

Their homes can be found underground, under rocks or even built above ground using materials like twigs, stones, or sand.

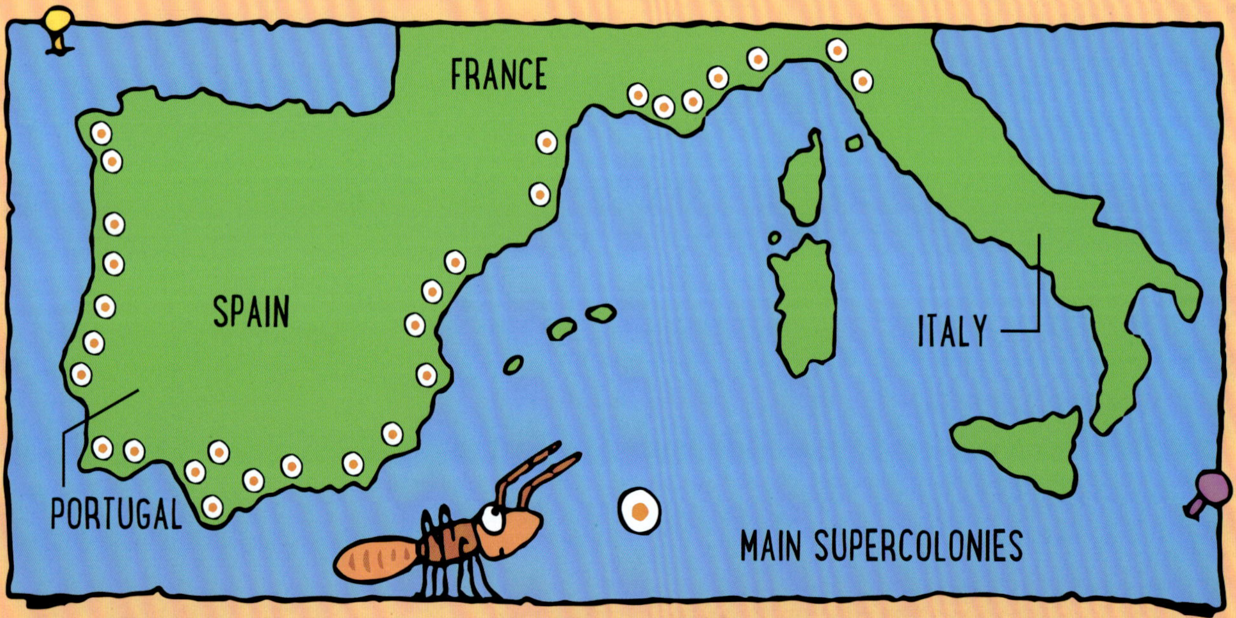

The largest ant colony in the world is the Argentine ant supercolony.

This massive network is made up of **millions** of nests and **billions** of worker ants spread out over a mind-boggling **3,700 miles** (6,000 km). You won't find it in Argentina, but it spans an area in the Mediterranean from northern Italy through southern France, then all the way to the western coast of Spain and Portugal.

Weaver ants are the team-building experts of the insect world. Once scouts find suitable leaves, they call for reinforcements. Hundreds of weaver ants then set to work, cutting and folding large leaves and gathering smaller ones.

In a coordinated effort, groups of ants come together to bend the leaves into shape and hold them in place. A new team of ants arrive with larvae in their mouthparts. The larvae release a strand of silk, which the ants move back and forth to weave the leaf walls together. Some large weaver ant nests can be made up of almost **300** leaves!

The world's largest hornet's nest is a work of art! A nest **16.5 feet** (5 m) wide in the shape of Mount Fuji was created by sculptor Yoshikuni Shiozawa and contains over **160,000** Japanese yellow hornets!

Wild honeybees are known to build hives in a variety of places, from rock crevices and hollow trees to underground burrows and even dried horse droppings. But how do they construct these intricate structures?

1 A worker bee consumes **honey**, which is then converted into **sugar** inside her body.

2 This liquid material is released through pores in her **abdomen** and mixed with **saliva** to create **wax**.

3 Using tiny mouthfuls of wax, the bees construct **hexagonal-shaped cells**, with an average nest containing around **100,000** individual cells.

Usually, the top cells in the hive hold honey, while pollen is stored in the middle section and **brood cells** are located at the bottom where young bees develop.

Each hive has one queen bee, who can lay up to **2,000** eggs in a single day. She shares the nest with thousands of female workers, and during the summer months, hundreds of male drones.

BATHTIME BUZZ!

Imagine this – you're showering peacefully and suddenly, instead of water, bees start pouring out of the showerhead! That's exactly what happened to a couple in Florida.

They discovered a massive hive **7 feet** (2.1 m) high hidden behind their bathroom tiles, housing around **80,000** bees. On the plus side, they also found **99 pounds** (45 kg) of delicious honey. Sweet!

WRIGGLY WORDS

Take a look at these helpful words from this book, which you could use when writing about brilliant bugs!

Annelid
A segmented worm

Antennae
Long, movable sensory organs on an insect's head

Arachnid
A group of arthropods which include spiders and scorpions. They have two body parts and eight legs.

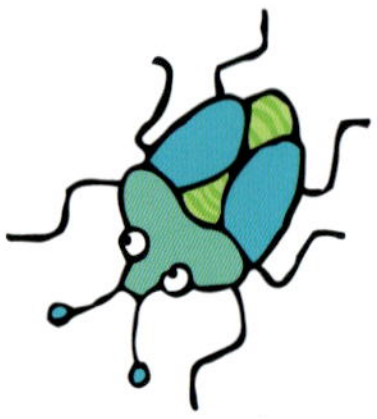

Calamistrum
A spider's leg bristles, used to comb silk threads

Chemoreceptors
Sensory receptors which detect smell and taste

Chrysalis
The pupa of a butterfly or moth

Cocoon
A covering around an insect larva, usually made of silk

Corbiculae
The container on a bee's back leg that is used to carry pollen

Entomologist
A person who studies insects

Entomophagy
The practice of eating insects

Exoskeleton
A skeleton on the outside of an animal. It supports the insect's body shape and protects its organs.

Hive
A nest of bees

Invertebrates
Animals or insects that don't have a backbone

Larva
The young wingless form of an insect that usually hatches from an egg

Metamorphosis
A process that sees an immature form transform into an adult insect in stages

Mollusks
Invertebrates that include slugs and snails

Myriapod
Insect with multiple segments, which include millipedes and caterpillars

Nectar
The sweet liquid which is given off by plants and flowers and collected by bees to make honey

Nymph
The immature form of some insects including mayflies and dragonflies

Photoreceptors
Cells in an insect's eye that respond to light

Pollinator
An animal that spreads pollen between flowering plants

Spinneret
An organ through which silk is produced

Thanatosis
When an insect pretends to be dead to avoid a predator

BUZZ QUIZ

Let's wriggle over to the Bug and Minibeast Quiz and put your knowledge to the test! The answers can be found at the bottom, if you're really stuck!

1. How many insects are there for every human on Earth?
A. 1.4 million B. 1.4 billion C. 140,000

2. What is the name given to people who study insects?
A. Entomologist
B. Crawlyologist
C. Flutterologist

3. How many legs do arachnids have?
A. 4 B. 6 C. 8

4. How long have insects been on Earth?
A. 480 million years
B. 48 million years
C. 4.8 million years

5. How many lenses does a dragonfly have in each eye?
A. 3,000 B. 30,000 C. 300,000

6. What are the receptors that help insects detect smells in the air?
A. Sentilla
B. Senpilla
C. Sensilla

7. How big is the African Giant Snail?
A. 1.5 in
B. 15.5 in
C. 153.5 in

8. Which insect can jump the farthest?
A. Toadtreader
B. Froghopper
C. Lizardleaper

9. Which predatory insect injects venomous saliva into its victim?
A. Assassin bug
B. Executing bug
C. Hit-guy bug

10. Which minibeast has the nickname "African Eye Worm"?
A. Auge auge worm
B. Loa loa worm
C. Ojo ojo worm

11. What percentage of crop plants need to be pollinated by animals?
A. 40% B. 60% C. 80%

12. How much honey is produced globally each year?
A. 1.9 million tons
B. 19 million tons
C. 190 million tons

Answers: 1. B, 2. A, 3. C, 4. A, 5. B, 6. C, 7. B, 8. B, 9. A, 10. B, 11. C, 12. A